PRAISE FOR QUIVER

"Such beauty as hurts to behold," wrote Paul Goodman. This magnificent book is like that. There's an almost Greek sense of fatedness in these poems, of the inevitability of blood relations leading one, not just to disaster, but to cruelty and moral pollution. Maybe you didn't grow up in a family like the one in this book. I did, so let me assure you Luke Johnson got it right: the ferocious longing to pour understanding and generosity over their stories, to admit complicity, to intervene retroactively to protect something, to save someone, anyone. To smash beauty against the story again and again, trying to force it to alchemize into something that can be borne. Why should you walk this via crucis with Luke Johnson, as I'm passionately recommending? For some, to affirm a truth that you already know. For others, as the Greeks believed, to learn from tragedy what's required to be human."
—Patrick Donnelly

"*Quiver* is a rare creation full of song and scar, authenticity and Old Testament mythology, of emotional complexity and witness. In a world where empathy is under threat of erasure, these poems of prophetic violence and harmful lineages take responsibility for themselves and remind us of our own responsibilities to each other. These poems both define and push against the edges of our shared American experience. At its heart, *Quiver* paints a multifaceted portrait of personal and communal betweenness. These poems choose to celebrate everything they touch. Even their own ghosts. Even that greater truth that always remains just slightly out of reach, that he refuses to stop reaching toward."
—John Sibley Williams

"In *Quiver*, Luke Johnson's unforgettable debut poetry collection, he invokes The Old Testament, its fires, floods, and prophecies—to reckon with "all the ways a child drowns, like spiders trapped in spit." These are harrowing poems. Yet, at the heart of Johnson's unsparing gaze lies enormous compassion—for the ghosts that haunt him, for the child self who carried "scars without witness." *Quiver* is a work of glorious complexity—brutal, lyrical, shot through with images that stop you in your tracks. But more than that, these poems look deeply at the ways the sins of the father are visited on successive generations and move toward breaking the cycle."
—Ellen Bass

Praise for Quiver

"*Quiver* is the most visceral, haunting book of poems I have read in years. Johnson reimagines masculinity and is unafraid to unearth its dark elements, as father, son, and witness to the brutality and beauty in and around us. He writes, "Listen: When/I said boys have a storm inside,/this itch that fills our teeth, I/was sharing in secret. I meant/we have mothers who gift us ghosts,/our heads upon a trigger." This searing debut is a world of its own, built with fearlessness, tenderness, and grace. Take notice. Luke Johnson has arrived."
—Lee Herrick

"In Quiver, Luke Johnson's inventive eye and sonorous voice seek to "pry the past apart." These poems pursue an allusive quietude beyond trauma and tragedy as wide-eyed, we witness a bruised boy become a tender father. Johnson's impressive debut collection stares into sorrow, but doesn't leave us to linger there. Instead, we swallow the darkness so we can breathe in the light."
—Matt Rasmussen

"In Quiver, Luke Johnson's startling first book, the poems are singing when they are stinging, scalding as they serve up something wildly fresh, slap after exquisite slap. These poems show us how vulnerability bleeds, and what it sees when it does. There is no soft peddling this poetry, with its faith, its strife, and such uncommon artistry."
—Elaine Sexton

"In *Quiver*—which, implausibly, is his first full volume—Luke Johnson cements his title as the uncontested master of shadow. These unnerving poems are the rustle in a vast and unrelenting dark, they are both salve and injury to the body, they are numbing slap and uneasy solace. The poet trains your eyes upon things you never wished to see—and holds you there, with chilling narrative and fierce lyric, until terror gives way to beauty. Am I saying....? Yes, that's exactly what I'm saying—*Quiver* will change the way you see."
—Patricia Smith

QUIVER

Library of Congress Cataloging-in-Publication Data

Names: Johnson, Luke, 1981- author.
Title: Quiver : poems / Luke Johnson.
Other titles: Quiver (Compilation)
Description: First edition. | Huntsville : TRP: The University Press of
   SHSU, [2023]
Identifiers: LCCN 2023014064 (print) | LCCN 2023014065 (ebook) |
ISBN
   9781680033205 (paperback) | ISBN 9781680033212 (ebook)
Subjects: LCSH: Coming of age--Poetry. | Fatherhood--Poetry. | LCGFT:
   Poetry.
Classification: LCC PS3610.O36446 Q58 2023 (print) | LCC PS3610.
O36446
   (ebook) | DDC 811/.6--dc23/eng/20230421
LC record available at https://lccn.loc.gov/2023014064
LC ebook record available at https://lccn.loc.gov/2023014065

Cover design by Bradley Alan Ivey
Cover Image liscensed via Shutterstock
Printed and bound in the United States of America

Published by TRP: The University Press of SHSU
Huntsville, Texas 77341
texasreviewpress.org

QUIVER

poems

Luke Johnson

TRP: The University Press of SHSU
Huntsville, Texas

TABLE OF CONTENTS

III

§

To dad, my kids and the ghosts that nearly broke us.

(boys)

—for Smitty, Slick Nic, Dave and Mortimer

In a barn
choked by rusty tools
and ragweed

we stood
in a riotous circle

watching
fetal mice fill
their fresh lungs with air

when Smitty
behind a seductive grin

pulled a blade
from his back pocket

and began
to slice one down the abdomen
with ballpoint precision

each of us stone-silent
and cold

as Smitty unsnapped
the sternum

then moved toward
the heart

a porous drum
swelling in his fingers

I

Bagging Mallards

All I wanted was the feathers.
A wing or two to sow under mom's machine

and spread so the wind could carry
me out in the Heavens. A home. A body born naked

with daddy's drunk blessing, ushered up anguished
to sing. Not spit. Not flight ground down with

bludgeoned beak left all alone and still dripping.
I dripped. Swelled in baths to bear it again spilled

out opaque and yellow. Yellow sun flowers smelling
of meat. Yellow light when a train comes close. Yellow

a moon over mountains in Mexico a stone glossed
smooth in a sling. All I wanted was a mom without

wounds. Without whispers and want and secrets
scratching names in floors leaving their thumb nails

and hair. Their teeth. Their dirty drawers
with blood spots stained like sequins. How dare I: a bastard

dancing song in the sky's panorama. Go hide, little duck.
You're better off bit through. Or dead.

Rats & Manna

This poem
has a house on a slipped foundation

and a woman beneath
the porch with a wrench trying
to tie down the posts.

She's heavy-set
with small hands and bites
her lips until they bleed.

Above her, footsteps thud
and dust swarms. She admires

the way the refraction of light
comes close and whorls
when her hand moves through it.

Remembers her father
preaching and pacing the aisles
between pews

while her silent mother
flipped a black bible and wrote notes
gin on her breath.

These days all it takes
is a gentle gale to shake the house.

If you're standing
by the stove frying tilapia
and a storm gathers

and what follows that storm
are silk howls wrapped with rain

you'll feel your feet wobble
as the structure cracks like ship bows
shifts for balance.

This is a poem more than a house.
A poem about a woman who
fixes three plates for supper

who waits patiently for the back door
to hook and close

and the house to erupt
with laughter so loud

wood shutters slap
metal sconces shake.

But there are no footsteps here
no voices in the clearing

no lover's hand
moving the hair from her face
when she fights fever

or builds a fence
or ties down the house
so the earth won't swallow her.

This is a poem about prayer
about the loss of prayer

about rats who nest inside walls
and leave shit lined
from room to room like manna.

About two plates left
like offerings for a lover and son
she carried six months into light.

Numbers 14:18

I've never told you
how my father tied
a drunk man to a chair

and snapped the first four fingers
on his left hand.

How the moon—
a sickle soaked in milk—
hung center the window

cracked from frantic birds
and how, the man, his dad,

howled like a stray in the hills
the boys bragged of maiming.
You might be wondering

what happened to the fifth finger
his thumb

and whether it stayed straight
or faced a similar form of fracture.
But none of that matters.

In the time it'd take
to detail a thumb pried loose, I

could move from the shed
to the house
a quarter mile north,

where my nana
swirls thyme in soup

and sways her hips
to Stevie Wonder, John Prine.
How can she dance

when the dead crawl inside?
How can she dance

with a body branded,
owned by a beast, a belt
that blooms the tremors?

Believe when I tell you
the fifth was spared.

That my father
ran out of brandy
out of spite

stopped soothing with brass
sought light

and stepped out,
deeply hidden—an animal
crazed for water.

That he found in his search
an oasis

and there lapped stars
until shame clotted
concealed

spread like mange
and swallowed him.

Sometimes that's all
that it takes. One taste.
One. For deadwind

to enter and eat
the insides

of a boy of a boy of a boy of a boy
of a boy of a boy of a boy—

I'll talk sadness, sure,

—after Brandon Melendez

but not about my sister
alone in a closet
with a mouse and book
of matches. So, here
is a pick and pane of ice
to stab until the pond spills.
Here is daddy's cane
frayed from blunt force
and its serpentine slap.
Here is the cat kicked
crooked for clawing
mother's wrist. A Remi.
Brass knuckles. Silk
blouse sequined by moths.
Here is a fence post
snapped to a spear.
A rope. Sticky needle.
A tulip chewed into pulp.
And laughter, as if
it were lodged in a drain,
drowned, knotted with hair.

The Unnamed Garden

Here is where your daddy
threaded a knife
through the mother deer's belly

who bellowed
when your fingers found

the fawn
and pulled it, wilted
from the body's cave, both eyes

widened and still.
Where once, on a walk,

when fog had crept
its muddy swill over the flash
of flood lights, you hid

your face afraid
the Lord would spit, his right hand

raised to strike.
You, half-nude, cock
still throbbing wet,

having joined a woman
twice your age

and tasted
where the womb began, its brine
the beauty of cream, bent

like one before a whip
to pay your filthy penance.

13

You bad boy dumb boy you
never enough boy, you fed
the body what it craved

and cowered by the climbing rose
that choked the wooden trellis.

How dare you.

Didn't you hear
the woman weep, while wandering
out to find you,

her voice
like something slick and fraught

sought for someplace
to drink, a body to wear, begged you
in from the cold?

You cradled the fawn.
You offered it back to the snow

and your daddy said *here*
by which he meant sip, to swallow
the moon's graffiti.

floodghost

Mother couldn't manage
what sated me, so she prayed:
sought in silence
a substance that'd soothe,
something familial with grace.
I groaned. Broke bodies
over blacktop's pane, a bottom-
less well of blood. At seven
I smothered a frog and fed each leg
to my quivering sister
laughed while she choked out its skin. At twelve,
I pulled a pistol from under
the vacant shed and shoved
its shudder to a schoolboy's temple, teased
while he wept in his piss.
And yet all along a Psalm, a satchel
of prayer: song. Mother making
contracts with the sky, while I
tore its pages to light a fire, warm
my hands around it. Radiant blue. Red
from a faraway pine.

Tabitha Road

The first son fell from a branch
and broke his hip.
Dragged his steps

down empty roads   searching
for someplace to drink.
The second

found a woman twice his age.
Touched her
till she melted in the palm

of his hand
and pooled between his teeth.
He slipped on ice

and hit his head,
leaving him battered
with a brain badly swelled

and a name
no longer his own.
The third I can't remember.

But the fourth
the youngest
broad and beautiful   eyes emerald flints

lived beneath the floor
listening to opera
and could be heard at noon practicing

his own pitch-less verse   a void
by which the birds banished,
and magnolias

16

divorced their blossoms.
Snow swept months
over rows of barns

and fields that sprouted
barley, and corn whittled
to feckless spears.

After the freeze,
when the melt was gone
and wild lupine leapt

from creases of sand   I watched
the mother set a table
with quail and pickles

and whistle her boys in the yard.
None of them came   not one.
And the mother

dressed in red   reached
as though a plate were passed
nodding her head in thanks.

She ate and laughed
drank and laughed   shimmied
to the small pond nude, then submerged

herself in sequined wakes
to mimic the motionless clouds.

Hum

An El Camino
bumps Beastie Boys
in a parking garage,

when two
broad-shouldered dudes
emerge from flickering barrel flames

and lumber
like vagrant shadows.

They jab
each other's ribs   talk shit

brag about the pussy
they'll crush later at the L,

then laugh
while bagging a beer.

                    The man in the car
                    is my dad's friend Jacob.

                    He's high on H
                    and learning to cope
                    with flashbacks

                    of boys blown open—
                    insides scattered by birds.

                    Jacob doesn't know now
                    is the moment he'll die.
                    The moment

                                        a gun he's shined
                                         from boyhood

                                   will erase puddled light
                                     and spill it like silk
                                        from his lips.

He pulls the pistol
from the front dash,
spins its chamber,

glides blurred vision
down the gun's oil-slicked
exterior, snaps it shut.

Scans the boys.
Frames their faces
as they approach the car quietly.

One taps the window,
while the other draws a light.

How much you need?
All you got, he says

                                   flashing back to the first
                                      buck he narrowed
                                   through a scope as a boy.

                                   How the crowned beast
                                      wobbles jack-lit pine
                                   like a lopped ballerina,

                                      how he holds it under
                                      till the kicking stops.

Like a Fish Gasping

Did I tell you a boy was walking home from school when a woman asked him if he'd like a cup of juice?

Did I tell you Jonah heard his mother's voice and muted her concern?

Did I tell you the woman grew angry began to weep threatened to follow him home?

Did I tell you Jonah ran?

Did I tell you she set her three dogs loose to harm him?

Did I tell you Jonah found his home, but the back door was locked?

Did I tell you Jonah ran?

Did I tell you Jonah never said no that he found her offer kind and besides she was an elderly woman anyway?

Did I tell you the home was large with locked windows no dogs?

Did I tell you Jonah sat down his brow was warm he needed just a sip?

Did I tell you he had more than a sip?

Did I tell you as he drank his body began to wobble he fell he dreamed of fish fondled by blades?

Did I tell you he woke with bloody fingers?

Did I tell you he was my friend he loved fingers he liked to suck fingers?

Did I tell you Jonah ran?

Did I tell you he woke with his pants undone and a broom stick up his ass?

Did I tell you Jonah liked fingers?

I offered my fingers found pleasure strange pleasure felt shame I silenced the Lord.

Did I tell you I silenced the Lord?

Did I tell you I woke with a sheet over my mouth and Jonah began to piss?

Did I tell you I swallowed piss?

I gasped like a fish out of waves.

Did I tell you I swallowed piss?

Did I tell you Jonah ran never came home his body a house without windows?

Did I tell you Jonah ran?

Did I tell you he put a gun to his head and did what the whispers wanted?

Did I tell you it wasn't his fault?

II

Song of the Stillborn

I lifted a calf from the barn floor
and despite its mother's refusal
left it for the pigs. They would not gather,

would not come from their pens
to feed from what had been offered.

The cord was wrapped around the still-dripping calf,
tongue unraveling, torso spotted with vernix.

I could have bound rocks to its ankles
and trusted it to tumble into boulders, break open,
become food for bottom feeders.

I could have built a fire, body lifted by smoke.

I did neither. I fit it back in the warmth
of its mother's mucus, and rested its chin

on her swollen belly. I could have cut a seam
in the belly of that dead calf

and placed the cut to the mother's nipple
as if it could come alive there and feed.

§

That summer my son was putty in my hands.
He came from brackish waters,

eyes nested with terror. He came
as one comes wailing from resurrection.

I lifted him from my lover's breasts
and despite the voice inside me saying run
don't ever look back, prophesied prosperity,

likened his hunger with mine. Bit him by the heart
and smoothed the impression into a seamless dimple.

Believe me: I
did not take the mother in the holler
and put a bullet through her brain. She was no

longer milkable, yes, and her calf left
for the buzzards, yes,

but there's something beautiful about a body
picked down to its spine.

How it carries its shape.
How it softens over time.

A Dilemma

If you feel a voice
like a leech in your throat
& that voice
is your drowned brother's,
& from it you hear
come, come closer
from a field at dusk,
where every spring
a single cardinal drops from pines
to paint the dark
its plume a flash of fire,
do you recede into the swelling blur
to offer back the bird,
or torch it over fertile earth
to feed a dormant flower?

Jeremiah

This poem
has a house and a field

and behind the field

a feral grove
of olives and lemons,

where a woman
once laid a baby

on a stone
and sprinkled gas in its hair

wept as it rose into flames.

Her lover stood
a few feet back

begging a bucket
of water, anything,

but she bound
his lips with a kiss

and took his hand
swallowed

his sorrow in bed.

This is a poem
more about rain.

About the sudden gales
that woke

in the field
and shook the house

threatened
to tear it away.

How the woman
would not

wake from sleep
as hail cracked windows

ripped through fence

rattled the backdoor
with rage. And how

her lover—a man
no older than forty—

fell on his face
and begged his boy

back from sky.
How the boy

would not come
how sky

would not answer
how light

was left swallowed
in the static of rain.

How a rope and a rafter
and a chair kicked loose,

brought him his sweet Jeremiah,
swaddled in cloth

and still kicking.

Finch

My son swats a finch with his bat
and laughs

when my daughter swoops
the breathing bird in her arms

and runs toward the river.
There, she stitches

the bird's torn wing with staples
and hangs it to a tree. All day

she speaks
as if she's never noticed its shadow

swaying above the chanterelles.

§

I read of a boy in Birmingham
who set fire to barns along an empty interstate.

He trapped horses in stalls
and admitted, when questioned,

it wasn't the thought of the roof imploding,
but the flurry of ash thereafter.

31

§

I want to tell you
how my daughter

laid the bird in a wood box
and dropped a match.

How she wept
as its wings went up in smoke.

But bear with me.

A little girl's sorrow
is worth a hundred men's lives.

§

Sometimes, on a walk,
looking for butterflies or fallen fruit,

I'll send my son a few hundred feet
to scout,

and ask, when he returns,
whether the acreage up ahead

is worthwhile. If so,
we'll eat until our stomachs ache. If not,

I'll demand he go a little farther,
looking for fruit

without bruised ruts or flies, finch
in the foreground singing.

§

Last summer
a wildfire gnawed spruce
to snapping tinder. Silence lumbered

the sky's carved dome
and came closer. At night it swelled
the blurred interior

like a lung of light. I'd wait
by the window, watching, wait
until sunrise. Listen for sounds

of my son's feet
racing across the cloven field, forbid
him to pass through the gate.

The Undoing

Jacob leaves a stick of sage
        smoldering on an abalone
                ashtray & skims his hand
                        across a bath filled with dahlia

their copper flames sinking
        as the steam furls them under
                like smashed faces
                        & fastens them to the tile.

He thinks of the boy he beat
        with a stick by the barn
                the boy who nearly died
                        the day his daddy found

him fondling men
        beneath the bleachers
                for forty dollars
                        & tied him to a tree

all night in wretched rain,
        the river frothing close.
                Jacob unsnaps his belt
                        unties his boots, pulls

his pants below the waist
        & stands in front
                of a foggy mirror
                        to hold his flaccid cock.

He slackens his jaw
        teethes his tongue
                mutters the name
                        of the boy who begged

barely able to breathe.
　　　　Outside the snow has fallen
　　　　　　& the sky chalked
　　　　　　　　& black ice barreled

stubborn dogwoods, rooting
　　　　for warmth underfoot.
　　　　　　Jacob empties himself.
　　　　　　　　Submits into the salted bath

to freely float unbodied
　　　　& begins to weep, his
　　　　　　wails a wounded mare.
　　　　　　　　The sort that goes on & on

as it's picked apart by birds
　　　　then spilled into
　　　　　　the sequined snow
　　　　　　　　the wind a volley of echoes.

Dead Man Walk

When Jacob lost his leg & went blind
four days from a bomb in Hanoi, he
saw visions of his sister. At five years
old in Pittsburgh, he found his mother
hung from a leash in the parlor
& tickled the tops of her hardening feet
to tease her out from the silence. When
she wouldn't wake, he put his ear to her
belly to listen for sweet Cecilia. When
Cecilia wouldn't stir or kick & his mother
started to stink, he went downstairs
to wait for his father & gaze out into
the snow. Dusk-blue faded tangled periphery
& a buck crept quiet from flowerless pine
pacing for somewhere to drink. Jacob admired
how it darted the dark, moved without
denting the snow, & started to shout there
in that glittering quiet to shake off sleet
from the window. When Jacob lost his leg

§

& went blind four days from a bomb
in Hanoi, he laid alone beneath the wreckage
feeling for his face. A mile from where he lay
dying, cherry trees lined a long narrow road
lifting their sweetness toward Heaven.
It was all a dream a vision, his hearing gone
left leg snapped in two, when a song began
to slice his sight & sift down slow from his
sister's lips, to wake him out of his slumber.
She said get up & he did—her skirt like skin
in mud—& the two of them followed
the river's ridge, wading through jungled briar.

Little girls playing with dolls in gardens, froze
while watching him near. They said *người chết
đi bộ* meaning "dead man walk" & streaked
to hide in sugared shade, afraid of what he'd
do. Their laughs like his sister's, the one he
still heard—high & perfect & small. Her green
eyes his. Her hair so blonde when she leapt
from trees, it flashed like coiled flames.

Witchery

—Bali, Indonesia

I wore the white batik and flat sandals
and walked the jungle road

looking for the pillar with the bell.

I happened upon a blind woman
throating guttural

like my friend Jack that night at church

when his jaw unlocked
and eyes rolled back

and every evil snapped inside his barreled chest

causing his voice to froth and throb
and sinew fat blue and veiny

like the woman begging the invisible

to twist out from gypsum sand
and braille along the bamboo floor

a warning about my future:

No go here. You, no go.
Winds do bad things.

Ramda come clicking from sugarcane

howl inside your blood.
Give me money L...

though I never told her my name.

Spit

Gin with quail eggs
Gin with butter
Gin with salted biscuit
and bacon fat,
made daddy want
to touch my hand
and take me in the canyon
to shoot skeet
and slur at fattened geese.
Made him want
to wash his feet in the river,
and wade
until his body'd lift,
drag downstream
and snag storm debris.
Once, plucking feathers
and dripping a dead bird dry,
he made me
put my hand inside
and pull the heart
place it under my tongue.
It snapped and quivered
dissolved in spit—
withered
and the winds laid down.
The canyon suddenly quiet.

Parakeet

My daughter dreams a parakeet falls from an iguana's mouth, screams
to be woken. I shake. Lift her limp from covers and lay her in a bath
with lavender oil. Darling, I whisper, Why again?

The pastor warned to send a spirit-shadow out, brings seven more. Seven rowdy guests with needs like lantern flies. I didn't listen: Let a witch prick the place where spirit found solace, steady drip, then braced for impact: windows slamming shut.

This is what happens when a father disobeys: winds braid violent in the den of her belly, bloat until she can't hold down water. She fevers. Buzzes like hornets swarmed under foot, bites down hard on your hand.

The doctors say the seizures start when she watches too much television. Something about shadows and light and the way her pupils recede and expand, synapse stuffed with halos.

I wrap her in a towel and rock where the window's blackened. Remember her dancing a field of dahlia, orchard laden with fruit. This before flies before fevers before her body a temple that ruptured and burned the Lord a liable witness.

Tomorrow she'll watch her brother leap from branch and break his leg writhe when doctors reset it. Weep. Pull from her pocket a dead parakeet point when its head hits the floor.

Larkspur

Just when
I think
the sky

has sloughed
its skin

so that breath
becomes untenable,

a hummingbird
stabs

the bluest
blossom, swivels
its beak to sate.

Behind the feeder
my daughter
spins

with both palms
raised, psalms
the blanched sky

Rain.

She's been
doing this for hours.

Rain.

Slaps a stick
to shriveled squash

to watch
its insides seep,

and swears
that when
the aphids' plume,

they pop
like peppered corn.

Love, I say

and she stops,
comes closer:

scribbles her name
on freckled window, spits
then smears it away.

Come inside.

To which
she nods no.

To which
she calls down
braids of bees

to interstate beauty
and bear it.

I am speaking
of sorrow.

Of a hummingbird
working rapid wings
in search of just a sip,

and this little girl
dizzy, pulling up brick,

begging
for larkspur
          mint.

As the body breaks, it is whole,

—to M

or so the silent Buddhists write
when describing why children die

beneath burning rubble made
from war machines. I wish I was the father

who fought harder for peace,
who believed I too could trade

collective pain for promises. Pilate
withered when the chants

of three hundred crazies called
for Christ's head. The night before,

his wife witnessed a warning
in a dream, and came to him crying

Let the rabbi go. I go into grocery
stores followed by ghosts. My father, once,

in an empty aisle, looking for frozen
cheesecake. My friend the next

with holes in his head, mopping
up spilled milk. M, why are the dead

so demanding? Why, when Christ
was nailed to die, did his mother

watch the thorns woven, her son
a slaughtered lamb? Listen: When

I said boys have a storm inside,
this itch that fills our teeth, I

was sharing in secret. I meant
we have mothers who gift us ghosts,

our heads upon a trigger. We're
bred to die. We're set

upon a foreign field
and asked to praise the blood.

Move in the world, my daughter

and mirror
the sound a robin makes,
when weaving string

to scabbed branch
but struggling to finish her knot.

Believe me, love
the world is cruel,
and the sky, though silent
filled with terrors, swarming
the swill of your voice.

I am worried.
To tell you this surely
will smother your song,
turn its glitter to soot.

But what do I know?

I walk like one
on ten-foot stilts, afraid
if I don't the dead will wake,
and make of my breath
a fading impression, a blemish.

That I will be
the thing forgotten,

as days turn over nameless hours
and roll among weeds

like wild harps,
like chalk dust thrown to wind.
O darling,

when I say sit, please stand.
Do not heed my monstrosities.

Run toward silos stitched
with rust

and climb them so
the light which slats, mimics
the rain's staccato.

Shout loudly, sway
and bare your teeth.

Cry by creeks
where prey seek shelter
and lullaby there.

Ladle the spark
that leaps from their fur
when rifles ravage them low.

This is what it looks like, son,

so stop stabbing the heron's belly,
as if repeated stabs

will wake it from the flies.
I mean what I say, when I talk
of permanence like permafrost,

or ancient arteries
of the earth's underbelly
spilling from volcanic pores.

A woman, did you hear?
Crated homing pigeons

and biked them
to a Tokyo market,
when her tire hit a rut

in the road
and the cage fell loose.
Nine birds died on impact,

while her most treasured—
still alive—but blinded

by headlights,
floated up over traffic
and faded into night.

For months
the poor woman wore grief
like a wet wool coat

and wept through
the deadwind of winter.

53

She'd set the table
each evening for two.

Wait for the backdoor
to swing and shut
and the sulfuric smell of sorrow

to come in the kitchen to eat.
Tristessa, she'd whisper,

and the ghostly girl
locked behind thick black bangs,
would look to her left and say nothing.

When I was a boy
I had a habit of carelessly sloughing bark
from a Eucalyptus. I loved its salve and

layered it like glue
over every burn left by my father's lighter.

And though that tree numbed each wound,
resulting in an able-bodied boy, one who'd go on
to live like most other boys,

I carried with me two things:
scars without witness and the tree's sick tinder.

Winter stars chafed into years of dissolution
and worms hollowed its core. Violent winds blew.

The old tree tilted,
fell loose from soil, then split in half.

For months, it ghosted an aroma so thick
the fallow fields became places to pray, rub
wounds and feel cleansed. I felt cleansed.

Opened my mouth
and ran nude in the rain. Its fading
ointment, coating my throat and my tongue.

Which leads me here with you, son.

This heron, no different
than the three-dozen floating out over the estuary,
was once a winged creature

maneuvering winds
with precision. It was effortless. Swooping

soft beach for sand dabs
then arrowing back toward light.

It's sick, I know, how
Man manipulates beauty.
But listen, son, listen:

I'm asking you
to set the weapon down
and look toward the Pacific.

That storm coming close,
is big enough to rip this beach and swallow it.
High tide will swell and splash

over the barriers
built to guard the street.
Perch will fill medians like manna.

The poor will come collect their rations.
Wave hands toward thunder and praise it.
I'm asking whether you'd

like to keep gazing at records of lost time,
or undress and wade these choppy waters—
bodies weightless as breath.

III

Winter Light

Let's say you watch your father
heave and sputter
and froth as air has left his lungs
leaving him still and small.
Let's say despite
your sisters' call home
your wife's call home
your children calling out for you
you've come to a bench
by a boarded-up gas station
to light a smoke
and stare across a shady brook
toward mountains plated in snow.
Let's say a mother swallow slaps
a passing truck
and flips across the sleeted street
landing alone in the gutter.
That as she fights you scan her eyes
and for a moment
find yourself inside your father's
childhood home
where winter light leans upon
a covered piano
powders an empty gun
then moves along the wooden floor
to fill a box of moths.
You place your lips upon
the swallow's beak to blow.
Watch its pebbled plume bloat
like a black balloon.
And remember how you'd
run the grove without your shoes
to climb the leaning oak
and listen for the egret's wings
in search of fields with water.

It was simpler then. Fire.
Snow. Flood. Sky. Hours falling
like flowers. Your mother
in her lavender slip looking
for wild honey
and both your sisters' parted mouths
longing for the rain.

When my daughter, not yet five

turns to study the contours of my face & says
I see you, says: *how long before the stars burn out*

which startles me, morphs her hands to hardness
a variable chill, I say *never*, say: *sometimes all we*

have is this & turn her toward my chest to spare
confusion. I fear of course the world

& cannot stomach sorrow, all the ways a child
drowns like spiders trapped in spit. I read a story

of a simple priest who stopped to sleep in a garden
at noon, & woke beside a wolf in snow who curled

to keep him warm. The day before, the priest
paused to praise an opening dahlia, & placed

its blue flame in his hair while undressing
by a stream. Sequined light, shadows of spring

clouds smeared by wind, he washed beneath
the Spanish moss & watched the flower fall

away—his secret lost to sin. When the dream
was over the wolf was gone & the priest began

to weep. When my daughter touched my fearful
face, I too began to weep. I read the story alone

in a room of a church made blue by rain. My
mother moved among its worn pews wiping

away the dust. We were poor & without grace.
I was without grace & groaning with blue. On the walls

the children hung papered stars, wrote prayers
in sparkled paint. One of them asked the Lord

for a pony, another for a million bucks to rebuild
Noah's ark. But one of the stars was without name

its prayer crossed out with blue. My brother
hiding. The boy without a spoken name who

plays a quiet cello.

Deadwind

There must be sea, gunmetal sky.

There must be gulls
plucking flesh from beached seals

and carrying the carcass to their young.

A drunk woman stumbling
in head-high surf.

There must be kite string

snapping when the line lets out.
A boy's cry. A mother's

sobering concern. A father

from a distance with a cigarette.
One hand strangling

the neck of a bottle, the other

rested flat on a dog with skin disease.
There must be a black umbrella

always an umbrella

even when it's warm, an umbrella
a feeling like an umbrella

a sadness, sand in the gums.

There must be bark stripped
free by homeless.

Burn barrels. Braided smoke.

A fight. A drunk woman
stumbling in head-high surf.

A father from a distance

with a cigarette.
One hand strangling a neck.

There must be a moon

red sickled
and a wind that deadens

the way breath deadens

when cloaked with ash
so much falling ash.

And this boy, frightened boy.

Charting a route from here,
to someplace in heaven.

The Boys of Cass and Pacific

—For Harmon

We lobbed a ball above a rim we could not reach.
Reached as though our feet

could find a rhythm right
with summer haze and black top, bodies
yet to stretch. Afternoons,

our daddies smoldered pipes on porches
playing cards, and stacked unemployment checks.

We dared not interrupt their count.
Dared not take a moment's glance
from men who mangled skin with brass

and bragged on corners filled with swagger,
swooping low to sweet ladies.

The things we did when no one watched
was worrisome: acid, shrooms, pop of bottles, bongs,
girls in jean skirts swaying hips

like nets in violet rain.
We learned to pass how to dribble how

to leap despite our average lift
and lilt like something holy wholly terrified,
shot clock clicking away. Years later, when the city

cleared the court we knew as boys
and the school no longer draped our names

our trophy trapped in glass, I watched an old friend
weave through traffic, stutter my name with surprise.

On his cheek a mark, one eye gone,

a limp and struggle for air.
He asked for a hit. Asked

if I'd ever been in love.
Wondered about my life my sons
if I'd lost or been slowly losing.

By which he meant light,
the lightness of air: the lob and lift and score.

The swelling crowd.
The flicker first before the bell
blaring into the night.

The Hive

Son:

Last night
I watched you steal a cig
and light it on the stove.

You slipped outside
to weave the smoke

and set it, flaring,
in a hive of bees,
to smother them softly

to sleep. First,
the workers
then the guardians,

then the queen
the last to quit, withered
into the wind.

I yelled,
but you would

not heed me, threw stones
but you did not care. You, who
thrashed with knuckled fists, fought

hard to stay with womb,
what called to you there?

What carried on
into the amethystine mist,
wooing you out for its pleasure?

69

Catalina

Alone on a boat
a mile off the coast, I
watched a glass squid
rise fluorescent
fold like flamed origami.
I thought of my mother,
dress blue, blurred
among the dogwoods,
thought of her hair billowing
laminate smoke
always an inch out of touch.

Liner Notes to Benjamin

Most nights our mother
made a gesture while she slept:

one hand balled in a fist,
while the other slapped the headboard:

she choked.

§

Too many times she'd
stroll a snowy dark

with eyes rolled back
in her head. Balance

a bridge rail to tempt
the wind,

mocking the body's balance.

§

Brother, come.

Spread snow along the floor
and shape your feet

in little indentations.
I'll follow you into the fields.

§

When I held my head
an inch under bathwater,

you crouched by the sink
with a frog in your teeth
both eyes puddled and stark.

Why did you smile
when I spoke your name,

spun from my whispers and fade?

§

Forgive the times I begged
because the wine was gone

and her hands began to itch
because I could not carry

your name. All she wished
was to touch your lips, turn

their tarnish to feathers.

§

We had these mittens:

booties woven blue
with lace like silken pearls

and this photo:

72

dad bearded, both hands
pressed to her belly—

one black kite
in a sky
beginning to smear.

To My Son Who Asks about Baptism

If you wake
and want to wash your feet

in a river,
reach above the baskets

in the bare garage
and pull from darkness

a folded flannel
to drape across your arms.

Follow where the stones
were pressed

and place your hand
on wire fence

to feel if rain is close.
Come to where

the road stops suddenly
and squint. Scan the space

between two poplars,
where swallows weave

to gouge persimmons
and a river carves

the canyon's sand,
drags behind drowned lures

fossilized trees
lamb skulls snapped

though smoothed. Listen:
If you want to wash

your feet in a river: don't.
Rise before the freight train

shakes the floor
and walk the fields

with blossoming hunger
to gather up wild berries.

Fill a bucket
with bleach and salt

and scrub the skins
to cut the tannins, cracking

them with your teeth.
Spit the husks

and scatter the seeds.
Suck until the juice

runs down your chin.
Son, lay in the laps of lavender

and admire the grasses
that shadow and sway, sweetly,

when the rain erupts.

WTR

—to Dad, Uncle K, Fred and a few others

My father
flips flapjacks
from a gas grill,

while a few
of his friends

pass a joint
and bullshit stories
from the seventies.

I'm sitting
by the remains
of last night's fire,

listening to
smoldering mesquite
crawl deeper into dirt

its sizzle
like the grill

as it spits
and pops batter back
from dad's fingers.

Every so often
I rummage
through ruins
of charred bark

to rediscover
a blue flame
riffing like a flag.

I hover my hand
above it,
smile

as a blister
forms to an island
in the center of a scar.

Dad dances plates
of eggs and flapjacks
to the table,

rocking hillbilly hips
to Clapton's contagious solo.

He says: Come sit son,
here, by me, my beautiful boy,

moving a wrinkled
stack of *Playboys*
and a few bottles of Beam.

I rise to my feet
like white trash royalty,
demand they serve me my meal.

Dark

—for Malakai

If you come to where
the thorny pears grow
along the one-way road

and crouch beneath
the sticky shade
that draws out

spiders and wasps
and children playing
chase in the dying light,

you'll witness, if lucky,
the buck my father
failed to shoot

sip from fading streams,
and freeze when salt
winds finger oaks

that pearl loose supple
flowers. Soon the winds
will die

and the blossoms settle
and the leaves
will shimmer liquid bruise,

while geese grow wild
with drunken gossip
then capsize in the dark.

As a boy I placed
my palm on the belly
of a drowned mare

and marveled
as meat wasps
entered its eyes

to thrum with frenzied
feast. I thought of my
mother shoeless, shifting

the reeds,
the rasp of her call
as she chased a child

who moved through
darkling mirrors.

I held my brother's
name in my throat
and hid at night

when woken by birds
milling around the attic.
My mother liked

to tell me they were
angels swapping
nightly news,

their heavy wings
of light,
and if I craned my head

79

and listened real closely,
I could hear them swivel
sugar in tea and snort

when falling asleep.

                              In the steady dark
                              the crickets crack
                              the quiet with their

                              calloused acoustics
                              and you are thinking
                              now of loss. How

                              the body is a busy
                              depot where people
                              stop to share a secret

                              or write a letter
                              or weep for a lover
                              who's no longer near

                              to kiss their eyelids
                              closed. Is the sting
                              in your stomach

                              an unbearable storm,
                              have your legs
                              gone weak with regret?

                              Listen: If you climb
                              the Eucalyptus
                              by the ghost house

and sit on the high branch
studying robins,
you'll watch the mother

come at dusk to feed
her babies and float
above their mouths.

They will cock
their heads and cry
until the mother stops

to fall asleep,
one eye guarding the nest.
Your hands will itch

to squeeze, my son, snap
their necks and be
done with it.

But I'm warning you

not to. You will play
that image again and again
and your hands

will fill with want
again and again
and for forty years

you'll feel her hover,
asking for the dead.

§

Quiver

I slurp a sad boy's fingers
    nibble where the skin
        has peeled & pull him out

        to spin inside pond splash
    powdered light. I study
the soft flesh, nip to pry

the past apart. Salve
    the place his mother
        maimed, a map with oil

        & skillet, prayed
    while watching him squirm. Later,
a sip of soup lifted

like an impartation,
    I drool because the fat
        has fallen off the bone

        fondled my throat
    with fennel. Fennel & quail.
Quail & floodplain. Salt,

mistsilk, spit. Their
    fragile bodies bagged
        then hung to dry

        headless over drip
    pans. *Like this*, he says: spoon
in his scarred hand—quivering.

Acknowledgments

I am forever grateful to the following publications in which these poems have appeared: *Kenyon Review, Prairie Schooner, Narrative Magazine, The Florida Review, Thrush, Frontier, Diode, Radar, The Cortland Review, Nimrod, The Greensboro Review, Tinderbox, Palette, Valparaiso Review, The American Journal of Poetry, Asheville Poetry Review, Barren, Connotation, Night Heron Barks, Poetry Online, Heavy Feather Review, The West Review, Vox Populi, Chiron Review, West Trade Review, Louisiana Literature, The Inflectionist Review, The Shore, Limp Wrist, Cultural Daily* and *Misfit*.

An added thanks to the following prizes who placed this manuscript a finalist: The Jake Adam York Prize through Milkweed Editions, The Levis Prize through Four Way Press, The Vassar Miller Award through University of North Texas, and The Brittingham & Felix Pollack Prize through University of Wisconsin.

Many thank you's to Sierra Nevada University's MFA program, where I developed as a poet, and wrote a handful of these poems.

I am forever indebted to the teachers and mentors who took an intimate interest at every level, in both my educational goals and writing life: Patricia Smith, Brian Turner, Lee Herrick, John Murillo, Laura McCullough, George Cotkin, Christina Firpo, James Cushing, Anthony Koeninger and David Leary.

Thanks to my incredible friends and fellow poets and artists who've pushed, encouraged, stretched and believed in me throughout this book's journey: Kathryn deLancellotti, Dare Williams, Max Heinneg, Samuel Duarte, Jeff Alfier, Tobi Alfier, Grant Clauser, Frank Paino, Despy Boutris, Timothy Liu, Michael Schmeltzer, Andrew McFadyen-Ketchum, Lynne Knight, Patrick Donnelly, Elaine Sexton, Lynne Thompson,

Benjamin Garcia, Jordan Rice, Dexter L Booth, George Perrault, Kelly Michels, Sean Thomas Dougherty, Laure-Anne Bosselaar, Megan Merchant, Alexis Rhone Fancher, Christopher P Locke, Alexis Sears, Gustavo Hernandez, Kevin Patrick Sullivan, Tom C Hunley, Ed Pavlic, John Amen, Michael Mark, Luke Hankins, John Sibley Williams, Faylita Hicks, Shaun Griffin, Elisabeth Adwin Edwards, Chiwan Choi, Davon Loeb, Shamar Hill, Ben Aleshire, Christian Gullette, Ken Harmon, Jack Bedell, Robert Vaughan, Kimberly Anne Priest, Connie Post, Scott Ferry, Robert Carr, Dave McAbee, Pat Salisbury, Scott Sundvall, Alexandra Umlass, Robi Nester, Tyler Julian, and the list goes on and on and on. I'm blessed.

Deepest gratitude to my mom, two sisters, and our father, Garry Ray, for whom this book is both love letter and exorcism. I miss you, dad.

And to my dream team, my family, those who hold me up when I can no longer stand: my wife Ciara, and three babies: Giana, Malakai and Micah. I love you cellularly, eternally. This is all for you.

About the Author

Luke Johnson's poems can be found at *Kenyon Review, Pairie Schooner, Narrative Magazine, Florida Review, Frontier, Cortland Review, Nimrod, Thrush,* and elsewhere. You can find more of his poetry at lukethepoet.com.